BAIT FOR EVANGELISM

SESSION 4

EVANGELISM *and* **DISCIPLESHIP**

DR. AARON R. JONES
Foreword by Dr. Timothy M. Hill

Interfacing Evangelism and Discipleship

WORKBOOK

Bait for Evangelism

Dr. Aaron R. Jones

Interfacing Evangelism and Discipleship - Bait for of Evangelism

Copyright © 2018 by Dr. Aaron R. Jones

Printed in the United States of America

Published by Kingdom Publishing, LLC, Odenton, MD 21113

All rights reserved. No part of this book may be reproduced or transmitted in any form or by any means, electronic or mechanical, including photocopying, recording or by any information storage and retrieval system without written permission from the author, except for the inclusion of brief quotations in a review.

All scripture quotations are from the King James Version of the Bible. Thomas Nelson Publishers, Nashville: Thomas Nelson, Inc. 1972

Editor: Sharon D. Jones

Graphic Designer: Janell McIlwain – JM Virtual Concepts

       Tiara Smith

ISBN 978-1-947741-19-5

Table of Contents

Interfacing Evangelism and Discipleship SESSIONS 1

Foreword 2

Fisher of Men 3

To Catch the Fish 5

The Translation 7

Where is Your Pond? 10

The Gospel is the Believer's Net 12

Fishing Bait 14

    Bait #1 - Common Ground 16

    Bait #2 - Love 17

    Bait #3 - Breaking Bread 18

    Bait #4 - Community Event 19

    Bait #5 - Holy Spirit 20

About the Author

Contact Page

Interfacing Evangelism and Discipleship
SESSIONS

Session 1—**Introduction and Philosophy**

Session 2—**5 Principles to Encourage Evangelism**

Session 3—**Components of Evangelism**

Session 4—**Bait for Evangelism**

Session 5—**Methodology of Evangelism**

Session 6—**Church Planting Produces Evangelism and Discipleship**

Session 7—**Babes in Christ**

Session 8—**Components of Discipleship**

Session 9—**Evangelism and Discipleship Plan**

Session 10—**Spirit of Forgiveness**

Foreword

When God calls a man of faith and fortitude to a specific purpose in the building of His Kingdom, He uses an individual like Dr. Aaron Jones.

Feeling the urgency of the hour, Dr. Jones has shaped his participation in the FINISH Commitment by emphasizing the merging of evangelism and discipleship strategies to assist churches and individuals in their quests to effectively reach the lost. As Senior Pastor of New Hope Church of God, he is well-aware of what it takes to affect the Great Commission of our Lord.

Dr. Jones' desire is to instruct others on how to deliberately make an impact on winning souls and then discipling them for powerful Christian service. His all-inclusive approach will intrigue and provide the impetus for those willing to pursue the heart of God.

Interfacing Evangelism and Discipleship will change the course of your outreach!

Dr. Timothy M. Hill
General Overseer
Church of God, Cleveland, Tennessee

Fisher of Men

Fisher of Men

"And he saith unto them, Follow me, and I will make you fishers of men."
    Matthew 4:19

_____
_____
_____
_____
_____
_____

Additional Notes

To Catch the Fish

To Catch the Fish:

- What type of fish are you _____?

- What equipment is needed to catch the _____?

- How deep is the _____?

- What _____ will you use?

- We need to know where the _____ are.

Additional Notes

The Translation

How do we translate the same principles into evangelism?
- Who has God called you to?
_____
_____
_____

- We need to know the souls we are trying to catch
_____
_____
_____

- What resources do you have?
_____
_____
_____

- What is the extent of the darkness?
_____
_____
_____

The Translation
Additional Notes

Where is Your Pond?

Where is your Pond?

_____
_____
_____
_____
_____
_____
_____

Additional Notes

The Gospel is the Believer's Net

The Gospel is the Believer's Net

_____
_____
_____
_____
_____

Additional Notes

Fishing Bait

Fishing Bait

- Is any substance used to attract and catch fish?

Fishing Bait

- What are you going to use to catch potential disciples?

_____
_____
_____
_____

- What will be the attraction tool?

_____
_____
_____
_____

Bait #1

Common Ground

Common Ground

- What do you have in common?

_____
_____
_____

- Building a relationship

_____
_____
_____

- Remove walls in the life of the unbeliever

_____
_____
_____

Bait #2

Love

Love

- Genuine care shown

_____

_____

_____

- Jesus was moved with compassion.

_____

_____

_____

- The ingredient that followed Jesus' ministry for the lost.

_____

_____

_____

Bait #3

Breaking Bread

Breaking Bread

- So many things take place at a meal table

_____

_____

_____

- Buy an unbeliever a lunch.

_____

_____

_____

- Treat a family to dinner.

_____

_____

_____

Bait #4

Community Event

Community Event

■   Many unbelievers will not come to church, but they will come to an event at a church.

_____
_____
_____

■   Use an event to shine for Christ.

_____
_____
_____

■   Find innovative ways to present the Gospel.

_____
_____
_____

Bait #5

Holy Spirit

Holy Spirit

- Never underestimate the power of the Holy Spirit.

_____
_____
_____

- Continuous prayers for the unbeliever's heart.

_____
_____
_____

Additional Notes

About the Author

DR. AARON R. JONES serves as Senior Pastor of New Hope Church of God. Under his pastorate is New Hope Kiddie Kollege, Inc (Daycare) and New Hope Community Outreach Services, Inc. Dr. Jones also oversees New Hope Church of God Ghana (2 churches) and New Hope Church of God Uganda (3 churches).

Dr. Jones is an Ordained Bishop with the Church of God denomination and is the DELMARVA-DC District Overseer (16 churches). Dr. Jones serves on DELMARVA-DC's Regional Council, Ministerial Internship Program Board, Urban Ministry Committee, Finance Committee, and Chaplain's Board. He also serves on both the Church of God's International and DELMARVA-DC Ministry to the Military Board. In his local community, Dr. Jones serves as a Chaplain for the Charles County Sheriff Department. He also serves as Board Secretary for the United Ministers Coalition of Southern Maryland, Inc.

Being obedient to 2 Timothy 2:15, "Study to show thyself approved...," Dr. Jones received a Doctorate in Theology and Pastoral Counseling from Life

Christian University and a Doctorate in Christian Counseling from American Christian College and Seminary. He is a certified Pastoral Counselor with the International Association of Christian Counseling Professionals. He is a Life and Pastoral Coach. He is the former Executive Vice President of the National Bible College and Seminary in Fort Washington, Maryland.

Dr. Jones has published ten books and a soul-wining project that provide a biblical foundation for Christian doctrine and discipline. He has recorded a CD entitled, Peace in the Storm. He is the founder and owner of God's Comfort Ministries, LLC, which provides Christian literature, evangelism training, and spiritual guidance. He has appeared live on TCT Network; WATC-TV's Atlanta Live; Babbie's House (hosted by CCM artist Babbie Mason); and In Concert Today on DCTV. He has done radio interviews with Radio One's WYCB's program; The Praise Fest Show; and online with Total Prayze. He was featured on the cover of Change Gospel Magazine and interviewed on Promoting Purpose Magazine.

Dr. Jones not only serves God, but his country as well. He has served over 20 years in the Armed Forces. He is a retired Chaplain with the Army National Guard. He participated in both Operation Noble Eagle (2003) and Operation Iraqi Freedom III (2005).

Dr. Jones is happily married to the former Sharon Russell. He sincerely believes without her love, support, and encouragement, many of his goals would not have been accomplished.

Contact Page

Mailing Address:
150 Post Office Road #1079
Waldorf, Maryland 20604

Website: www.godscomfort.net

Email: drjones@godscomfortmin.net

Facebook: God's Comfort Ministries

Twitter: @GodsComfort_Min

Instagram: @godscomfort_min

GOD'S COMFORT MINISTRIES

God's Comfort Ministries (GCM) provides practical Christian books, teachings, trainings, and coaching to new converts and seasoned believers. GCM provides understanding of the doctrinal principles of the Bible.

Services Provided

Pastoral and Life Coaching

Evangelism and Discipleship Training

Spiritual Guidance

New Author Consultation

Christian Literature

www.ingramcontent.com/pod-product-compliance
Lightning Source LLC
Chambersburg PA
CBHW081358080526
44588CB00016B/2536